WONDERS OF THE WORLD

► Japan's Akashi-Kaikyo Suspension Bridge opened in 1998, linking the city of Kobe to Awaji Island. It has a total length of almost 4km and is designed to withstand winds as high as 285km/h and earthquakes of up to 8.5 on the Richter scale.

KFK KINGFISHER KNOWLEDGE

WONDERS OF THE WORLD

Philip Steele

Foreword by
Françoise Rivière

Assistant Director-General for Culture, UNESCO

KINGFISHER

Editors: Vicky Bywater, Miranda Smith,
  Hannah Wilson
Designers: Malcolm Parchment, Rebecca Painter
Consultant: Dr Miles Russell, School of
  Conservation Studies, Bournemouth University
Picture research manager: Cee Weston-Baker
Senior production controller: Teresa Wood
DTP manager: Nicky Studdart

GO FURTHER...
INFORMATION PANEL KEY:

websites and further reading

career paths

places to visit

KINGFISHER

Kingfisher Publications Plc, New Penderel House,
283–288 High Holborn, London WC1V 7HZ
www.kingfisherpub.com

First published by Kingfisher Publications Plc 2007
10 9 8 7 6 5 4 3 2 1
1TR/0107/TWP/MA(MA)/130ENSOMA/F

ISBN 978 0 7534 1426 2

Copyright © Kingfisher Publications Plc 2007

Printed in Singapore

Contents

▼ The Great Pyramid at Giza in Egypt is the only survivor
of the seven wonders of the ancient world.

NOTE TO READERS
The website addresses listed in this book are correct at the time of going to print. However, due to the ever-changing nature of the internet, website addresses and content can change. Websites can contain links that are unsuitable for children. The publisher cannot be held responsible for changes in website addresses or content, or for information obtained through third-party websites. We strongly advise that internet searches should be supervised by an adult.

Foreword

In ancient times, there were seven 'Wonders of the World'. These were places that were so beautiful, so unique, that they were considered to be the most extraordinary places in the world. Nowadays, only one of these places is left: the Pyramids of Egypt, with its famous sphinx. This is now a World Heritage Site.

In 1972, UNESCO adopted the Convention concerning the Protection of the World Cultural and Natural Heritage. This is an agreement signed by 182 countries of the world. Each country that signs this agreement makes a promise to protect their own heritage, but also to help other countries to protect theirs. To date, 812 sites have been recognized as places so important for the whole of humanity that they deserve to be protected by the international community as a whole.

There are many wonderful places around the world. Some of them are incredible achievements of human imagination and skill, for example the Eiffel Tower in my home country of France. In Tsodilo, Botswana, ancient rock-art drawings show us how people first used to communicate through art, and there are modern fantastic buildings such as Antoni Gaudi's works in Barcelona, Spain. This book looks at many of the wonders that have been built by people through the ages. There are also extraordinary natural places, from the brightly coloured corals of Australia's Great Barrier Reef to the tropical rainforests of Sumatra, Indonesia, or the vast plains of the Serengeti in Tanzania. Sometimes these are only home to certain animal and plant species, so it is essential that we keep them safe as well.

If we do not take care of these magnificent places, they will disappear. That is why it is important for all of us to know about them and find out how to protect them.

What is the heritage of your country? You probably know about Stonehenge, the stone circles where Druids used to meet, or the amazing fossils of the Devon and the east Dorset coast. Do you know that similar stone circles are World Heritage Sites in Senegal and Gambia, and that the earliest human fossil site is located in South Africa?

You can learn about the heritage that is near you, and you can visit and see for yourself. With the help of this book and the links it provides, you can also find out about places that are important to peoples of other countries. The better we know a place, the better we will care for it in the future.

Françoise Rivière
Assistant Director-General for Culture, UNESCO

BLACK SEA

Greece

Temple of
Artemis, Ephesus ●

Turkey

Statue of Zeus,
Olympia ●

Mausoleum, Halicarnassus ●

Colossus, Rhodes ●

Iraq

Hanging Gardens, ●
Babylon

MEDITERRANEAN
SEA

Pharos, Alexandria ●

Great Pyramid, ●
Giza, Egypt

Egypt

CHAPTER 1

The seven 'Wonders of the World' were all in the same
area of the world – on or near the Mediterranean Sea.

Seven ancient wonders

Tourism is nothing new. More than 2,000 years ago, Greeks and Romans were travelling to far lands including Egypt to see the sights. They visited monuments such as the Great Pyramid of Khufu, which even then was more than 2,500 years old. Travellers boasted about their voyages, telling tales of the amazing things they had seen. The Greek writers Herodotus (484–420BCE) and Callimachus of Cyrene (305–240BCE) wrote lists of these wonders. A poet called Antipater of Sidon, who was writing in about 120BCE, drew up a chart of the top seven attractions. Through the Roman period and the Middle Ages, writers became fascinated with the seven 'Wonders of the World', and those of the ancient world are now established. But the idea of choosing wonders is something that is still popular to this day.

The Great Pyramid

Today, three massive stone monuments tower over the desert at Giza, near the modern Egyptian city of Cairo. The largest of these is the Great Pyramid, which was sited between the River Nile and the Western desert, and built over a 20-year period, finishing around 2560BCE. It contains the burial chamber of Khufu, a pharaoh of Egypt who died in 2566BCE. Visitors to the Great Pyramid today are still struck with awe. Imagine how it must have looked when it was first built, covered in shimmering white limestone and capped with gold.

▲ Near the Great Pyramid is a statue with the body of a lion and the head of a man. Its face probably represents the pharaoh Khafra, who died in 2532BCE. This mysterious monument has fascinated people for more than 4,500 years.

Built on a gigantic scale

A true pyramid has a square base, from which four flat sides converge to a point. The Great Pyramid was originally 146m high – it is shorter today because its topmost stone is missing – and the base measured 230m from corner to corner. The word 'pyramid' is Greek, not Egyptian, and it is named after a small wheat cake that the Greeks used to bake in much the same shape. It hardly seems a suitable word for such a massive structure. This pyramid was made up of over two million stone blocks, each averaging 2.5 tonnes in weight.

◀ The Great Pyramid was surrounded by temples and smaller pyramids. Later, two other great tombs were added to the temple complex, the pyramids of Khafra and Menkaura.

▲ The earliest form of pyramid in Egypt had stepped sides. This was the tomb of the pharaoh Djoser, at Saqqara. He died in 2648BCE. The core of the Great Pyramid was also stepped, but it was finished by filling in the steps and covering the surface with limestone, to make smooth, flat sides.

Working for the pharaoh

Giza must have been one of the biggest construction sites in history, thronged with architects, masons, surveyors and many thousands of toiling labourers. All sweated under a blazing sun. The man-made mountain may have taken up to 20 years to complete, and there were temples and riverside piers to build as well. The work was not carried out by slaves, but by thousands of ordinary citizens. They were expected to offer their services to the state each year when floods on the River Nile forced them to stop farming for a few months.

A boat to eternity

When Khufu died, his body was carried by boat across the River Nile to the temples of Giza, and then sealed inside one of three burial chambers in the Great Pyramid. The Egyptians believed that the survival of their whole world depended on the pharaoh travelling successfully to the afterlife – the pyramid was in effect a giant launching-pad for the spirit of the dead ruler. In fact, Khufu did gain a kind of immortality, for his tomb ensured that his name would live on. For thousands of years, the Great Pyramid remained the world's largest and most famous building.

Marvels of Babylon

Babylon was one of the world's first great cities. It lay at the heart of Mesopotamia, a region of western Asia that covered much the same area as modern Iraq. Babylon is often mentioned in ancient Greek lists of the seven wonders. Most writers praised the legendary 'Hanging Gardens' of Babylon, but others were more impressed by Babylon's massive city walls.

◄ It was said that the ruler Nebuchadnezzar II built the Hanging Gardens for his wife Amytis. She was from the green mountains of the northeast and was weary of the dusty plain around Babylon. They both loved to wander along the lush terraces of the gardens.

Cradle of civilization

Mesopotamia has been called the 'cradle of civilization'. It was here that the first towns and cities in history were built, that laws were first drawn up, that the world's first empires were created. Mesopotamians invented writing, the 60-minute hour and the wheel. Babylon, already a city of some 200,000 people, became the centre of a great empire in the 18th century BCE. It had another great period of power after 625 BCE, and it was this second empire that was so admired and talked about by Greek travellers.

► The word 'paradise' originally meant a walled garden. Gardens were greatly valued in ancient Mesopotamia and Persia and were laid out around many royal palaces. In a hot, dry land, tinkling fountains and shady pools seemed to be the ultimate luxury. As the Babylonian empire became ever larger, all sorts of palms, exotic shrubs, luscious fruits and fragrant flowers might well have been brought back for planting in Babylon's Hanging Gardens.

The age of Nebuchadnezzar II

Babylon was built beside the River Euphrates, which provided precious water in what was a dry region. Over the city towered a sacred monument, a huge ziggurat or stepped pyramid. Babylon was also the centre of trade, jewellery-making, weaving, astronomy, mathematics and learning. The city was rebuilt by the powerful king Nebuchadnezzar II, who reigned from 605 to 562BCE. The outer wall of his new city was 18km long and 24m thick. Its gates were glazed in blue and decorated with mythical creatures. A war chariot could turn on top of the wall – and that alone made it a wonder of the world for some Greeks.

The Hanging Gardens

The Greek word *kremastos* actually means either 'hanging' or 'overhanging', and it is likely that the gardens on terraces 'overhung' the city. But were the terraces of the city really planted with exotic trees and vines, and flowering shrubs? Some archaeologists claim to have found traces of the gardens, but others do not believe that they existed in the first place. The gardens are not mentioned in Babylonian records. Were the Greeks thinking of the palace gardens at Nineveh, instead? Perhaps we shall never know.

▲ Greek descriptions of the Hanging Gardens talk of concealed channels of water designed to keep the roots of the plants moist. The water wheel feeding buckets above may have been the kind of device used to drive water through the concealed channels. Mesopotamian civilization depended on irrigation, canal-building and water engineering. It was these skills, developed in the region over a period of thousands of years, that were so admired by the Greeks.

Olympic Zeus

Zeus was the king of the Greek gods, the lord of the sky. He was the bringer of justice, who hurled thunderbolts at wicked humans. In about 430BCE, the Greeks erected a magnificent statue to Zeus that showed him in all his majesty and power. The statue was created by Phidias, the greatest of all Greek sculptors. It was placed in a temple at the sacred site of Olympia in southwestern Greece, which was the home of the famous ancient religious and sporting festival – the Olympic Games.

▶ The statue of Zeus stood in a temple that had been built in 457BCE. The figure of the god was about 12m high, and carved from ivory. His robes were of gold. In one hand he held a life-sized statue of Nike, goddess of victory, in the other a sceptre topped by a golden eagle.

◀ The ruins of the temple of Zeus may still be visited today. Olympia had been a sacred site for a long time and the goddess Hera was also worshipped here. Beneath the blue skies and hot sunshine, the dark groves of trees offered shade and peace.

The Olympic Games

Olympia was never a town in its own right, although it offered accommodation and places for visitors to eat. Travellers came to Olympia because of its famous games, which had started in 776BCE or even earlier. The games were a festival of athletic skills. They had begun just with running events and wrestling bouts, but eventually also included horse races, chariot races, boxing and racing in armour. Competitors came from all over Greece and from distant Greek settlements overseas. Successful athletes became very famous.

▼ On the front of the temple of Zeus, statues showed scenes from Greek mythology. Here, an ancient tribe called the Lapiths are battling with the centaurs, who are half-human, half-horse.

Honouring the gods

The Olympic Games were held every four years. They were the occasion for showing off physical prowess, and feasting and drinking. Only men could attend, although there were separate female games held in honour of the goddess Hera. Some 40,000 spectators could fit into the stadium. However, the Olympic Games were more than a sporting contest. They remained a deeply religious occasion and were primarily a religious festival held to honour Zeus, the father of the Greek gods and goddesses. None of the Greek states could go to war during the games, and sacrifices were made to the gods. It was only fitting that the king of gods should be honoured here.

▶ Throwing sports at the ancient Olympics included the discus (right) and the javelin. This lifelike statue of a discus-thrower in action dates from about 460BCE. Discus-throwing is still an Olympic sport today.

▼ More than 11,000 athletes from 202 countries competed at the 2004 Olympic Games, held in Athens, Greece. The spectacular closing ceremony in the main stadium was watched by around 70,000 spectators.

An end and a new beginning

The statue of Zeus at Olympia was hailed as one of the wonders of the ancient world. However, centuries later, when the Greeks became Christians, the old gods were frowned upon. Emperor Theodosius I banned the games in 393CE. By this time, the statue of Zeus had been carried off to the newly built Greek city of Constantinople (modern-day Istanbul). Sadly, the statue of Zeus was destroyed there by a fire in 462. However, the story does have a happy ending. The Olympic Games were eventually revived in 1896 and are now the foremost athletics contest in the world, held in a different country every four years.

Temple of the goddess

Foreign kings, merchants, pilgrims and travellers came from far away to see the Artemisium, the great temple of Ephesus (in present-day Turkey). They left gold, silver and jewellery there as offerings to the goddess Artemis. Visitors were awestruck by this splendid building, which seemed to reach to the clouds. Ancient writers reported that the temple was more impressive than the pyramids of Egypt or the city of Babylon. Some hailed it as the greatest wonder of the world.

◄ The goddess Artemis is shown here in the form in which she was worshipped at Ephesus. The wild animals indicate her role as a goddess of the wilderness and the hunt. Her bust is hung with what may be multiple breasts, symbolic of her role as a mother goddess.

A city by the sea

Today the eastern coast of the Aegean Sea is part of Turkey. In ancient times, it was the home of various peoples of the region. The Greeks settled here in around 1050BCE and built a city in Ephesus. This reached the height of its wealth in the 6th century BCE. For a time, Ephesus came under the rule of the Persian empire. Even before the Greeks arrived, the site of Ephesus had been sacred to a mother goddess called Cybele. The way in which Cybele was worshipped soon became mixed up with the ceremonies carried out for a Greek goddess called Artemis, and the Greeks built temples in her honour.

▼ In ancient times, the temple site was busy with traders selling items to pilgrims. On festival days, there would be sacrifices of bulls at the altar. Religious processions followed a sacred route that led from the town to the temple of Artemis.

The goddess

Building work on a new temple dedicated to Artemis was started in Ephesus in around 550BCE, and the building was completed around 120 years later. In Greek mythology, Artemis was worshipped as the twin sister of the sun god, Apollo, and was known as the 'lady of wild animals'. She was also the goddess of wild places. Artemis was often shown hunting, with a bow and arrows. In Ephesus, she was represented more often as a goddess of fertility and childbirth. The Roman name for Artemis was Diana.

Marble and fire

The base of the temple in Ephesus was 115m long and 55m wide. It was built of gleaming white marble, and its 127 columns were 18m high. In 356BCE, the Artemisium was burned down by a young man called Herostratus, who thought that this act would make him famous forever. The temple was rebuilt in around 250BCE, but it was destroyed again by the Goths, northern European warriors who raided Ephesus in 262CE. The last remains of the temple were torn down by Christians at the beginning of the 5th century CE. The site was not rediscovered until 1869.

▶ The bases of the temple's columns were made from marble, and some displayed beautiful carvings. Like most of the stonework, they would have originally been painted in bright colours. Other parts of the Artemisium were adorned with colourful paintings.

The Mausoleum

In the 4th century BCE, travellers sailing down the eastern coast of the Aegean Sea brought back tales of an awesome building. It was the tomb of a ruler called Mausolus and stood in the city of Halicarnassus. This memorial to Mausolus was called the Mausoleum, and it became so famous that, today, any tomb designed as a grand public monument also carries the name 'mausoleum'.

▶ Mausolus was a native of Caria. He governed the region at a time when it was part of the Persian empire. However, he rebelled against the rulers of the day, and managed to win personal control of Caria and neighbouring territories.

The life of Mausolus

Halicarnassus stood on the site of the modern town of Bodrum, in Turkey. The region, known as Caria, was home to the Greeks and other Aegean peoples. According to the royal custom in those days, Mausolus married his sister, Artemisia. Together, they created an impressive new capital city, in the Greek style, at Halicarnassus.

Mausolus and Artemisia set about building the most magnificent tomb the world had ever known. When Mausolus died in 353BCE, it was up to Artemisia to make sure that the project was completed as planned.

Artemisia's creation

As soon as they heard of her brother's death, the islanders of Rhodes rose up against Artemisia, but she crushed their rebellion. Then she made sure that only the very best Greek architects, builders, sculptors and craftsmen were employed to finish the tomb. It was located on a hill above the town and was completed in 350BCE. Artemisia died soon afterwards. Her ashes were placed in the Mausoleum alongside those of her brother.

The perfect monument

The Mausoleum was set on a massive tiered platform adorned with stone lions, and statues of gods and warriors. The marble tomb was decorated with images from Greek mythology, including centaurs (half-human, half-horse) and Amazons (female warriors). There were soaring columns and a massive roof, topped by a gleaming chariot of gold drawn by four horses. The tomb survived until the Middle Ages, but was then wrecked by a series of earthquakes. Rescued by archaeologists, parts of the tomb may still be seen today in London's British Museum.

◀ The Mausoleum above the town was about 45m high and had 36 columns, nine on each side, set around a central block which supported the stepped roof. The base measured about 40 by 30 metres. This beautiful memorial was part of an ambitious building scheme in Halicarnassus, which included a citadel, dockyards, city walls and many other monuments and statues.

▲ What impressed visitors to the Mausoleum most was the lifelike quality of its many statues and friezes. The stone-carved scene above shows a fierce battle between Greek warriors and Amazons, the warlike female race described in ancient Greek poems such as Homer's *Iliad*.

The Colossus of Rhodes

Sailors would gaze upwards in awe as their sailing boats entered the ancient harbour of the Greek island of Rhodes. Towering above them was a gigantic statue of Helios, the sun god. As the sailors squinted against the dazzling sunlight reflected from the statue's bronze casing, they could make out a crown of rays shimmering against the blue sky. The statue stood on a 15m-high marble base and was itself an amazing 34m tall.

▶ The Colossus was built by the sea, so that all visitors to Rhodes would be impressed. It was later said to straddle the harbour entrance, with ships passing between its legs. In reality, it was probably built to the east of the harbour. Swords and spears that had been abandoned by Demetrius' army were melted down and used in this new monument to peace. Abandoned siege towers were built into the scaffolding. The core of the structure was made of stone blocks reinforced with iron. The outer skin of the statue was made from plates of bronze.

War and peace

The story of the 'Colossus', the giant statue of Rhodes, began with a war. The islanders of Rhodes had made an alliance with the Greek ruler of Egypt, Ptolemy I. Another powerful ruler, Antigonus I of Cyprus, tried to put an end to this alliance by sending his son Demetrius to besiege Rhodes. In 304BCE, Demetrius was forced from the island and the islanders began their victory celebrations. They decided to ask the sculptor Chares of Lindos to commemorate the peace by building a giant statue of the island's most important god, Helios. Construction work took place between 292 and 280BCE.

The fall of Helios

Few travellers could ever forget Rhodes and its giant statue of bronze. A beacon could even be lit from the torch it held in its hand. All agreed that the Colossus was a wonder of the world. Sadly, it was toppled by an earthquake in about 226BCE, and lay on the ground in ruins for nearly a thousand years. The islanders refused to rebuild the statue because they believed they had offended Helios in some way and that he had caused the statue to fall. The remains of the Colossus are said to have been eventually sold and the bronze pieces carried to Syria on the backs of 900 camels.

◀ A coin portrays Helios, god of the sun, with his crown of rays. Helios was believed to drive his fiery chariot acros the sky by day, before sinking under the waves at sunset. A festival of Helios was held on the island, during which a chariot with four horses was driven over a cliff into the sea to symbolize the setting of the sun. The god was especially honoured on Rhodes, a tradition which may have come to the island from the Asian mainland, which lies just 16km to the east. It was said that the people of Rhodes were descended from the god's seven sons.

Pharos of Alexandria

Of all the wonders of the ancient world, only one served a practical purpose. This was the Pharos, a tall lighthouse that guarded the harbour at Alexandria, in Egypt. The city of Alexandria had been founded by the Greek leader, Alexander the Great, in 331BCE. One of the generals who fought with him became the Greek ruler of Egypt in 323BCE, taking the title Ptolemy I. Ptolemy ordered work to begin on this building project in about 290BCE. The tower was completed during the reign of his son, Ptolemy II.

▲ Ptolemy II, known as Philadelphus, was ruler of Egypt when the Pharos of Alexandria was finished. His father, Ptolemy I, had begun the project some 20 years before.

▶ Today, Pharos island in Alexandria is occupied by a citadel, which forms part of coastal defences built in 1480CE by the Egyptian sultan Al-Ashraf Qaitbay. Some of the larger stones used in its construction came from the original Pharos.

A landmark for sailors

To sailors travelling to Alexandria from Greece, the Egyptian coastline appears low on the horizon and often shimmers in a heat haze. Ptolemy I decided that sailors needed a navigation aid to mark the entrance to the harbour. He ordered the architect, Sostratus of Cnidus, to build a high tower on a small, rocky island called Pharos, which was joined to the mainland by a sea wall. Soon the whole tower became known as the 'Pharos'. After the Romans began to rule Egypt in 30BCE, the tower was transformed into the world's most famous lighthouse. The signal could be given out either be a dazzling mirror that reflected the rays of the sun or by a blazing beacon that was visible by night.

The tower tumbles

The Pharos was over 90m high and it was claimed that seafarers could see the light from the tower at a distance of more than 50km. It was made up of three storeys and built of stone blocks, which were later reinforced with lead. It was decorated with statues of Triton, the mythical sea messenger of the Greeks, and was later topped by a statue of Triton's father, Poseidon, god of the oceans (or possibly Zeus, father of all the gods). The great lighthouse stood for nearly 1,500 years, but finally collapsed into ruin during an earthquake in 1303CE. It was finished off by a second tremor in 1323, becoming the last of the six lost wonders of the ancient world to disappear.

▲ The Pharos was approached by a ramp and had a central shaft for fuel and maintenance. The lower section was square, the middle section was eight-sided and the top section was round. It was so famous that in many languages the word for 'lighthouse' comes from 'Pharos' – for example, the French word is *phare*.

▶ In the 1990s, marine archaeologists from France began to investigate the harbour at Alexandria. They found evidence from many different periods of Egyptian history, including some massive blocks of stone that probably came from the original Pharos. Some were inscribed with Greek letters. Here, diver Jean-Yves Empereur examines earlier underwater remains.

SUMMARY OF CHAPTER 1: SEVEN ANCIENT WONDERS

Helios the sun god, in whose honour the statue of the Colossus of Rhodes was erected.

The world of the Greeks

The ancient Greeks were great travellers. Their homeland lay in the region of the eastern Mediterranean. About 2,800 years ago, they also began to settle in many other lands around southern Europe and western Asia. By 323BCE, the Macedonian ruler Alexander the Great had led Greek armies across much of Asia and into Egypt as well. The ancient Greeks loved to talk and write about the incredible sights they had seen on their travels.

The writers

There grew up a fashion among Greek authors to list the seven places that they thought were the most wonderful of all. These writers included Herodotus (484–420BCE), Callimachus of Cyrene (305–240BCE) and the poet Antipater of Sidon, who lived in about 120BCE. A famous text called 'About the Seven Wonders of the World' was probably written in the 6th century CE.

The Seven Wonders

The list of Wonders of the World varied from one writer to another, although there is agreement about the following:
1 The **Great Pyramid** at Giza in Egypt was built for the death of the pharaoh Khufu in 2566BCE.
2 Babylon and perhaps its **Hanging Gardens** were in Mesopotamia (ancient Iraq). Babylon was certainly rebuilt during the reign of Nebuchadnezzar II (605–562BCE).
3 The majestic statue of the god **Zeus** at Olympia in Greece was erected in about 430BCE.
4 The **Artemisium** at Ephesus (now Turkey) was also completed in about 430BCE.
5 The original **Mausoleum** was the most impressive tomb of its day. It was built at Halicarnassus in c.350BCE.
6 The **Colossus** was a gigantic statue of Helios the sun god, erected near the harbour of Rhodes in about 280BCE.
7 The **Pharos** (c.290BCE) was a landmark and beacon marking the entrance to the port of Alexandria in Egypt.

Go further...

Read more about the seven wonders of the ancient world at:

http://ce.eng.usf.edu/pharos/wonders/list.html

Life in Ancient Rome by Simon Adams (Kingfisher, 2005)

Ancient Egypt: Eyewitness Guide by George Hart (Dorling Kindersley, 2002)

Ancient Greece: Peter Ackroyd Voyages Through Time by Peter Ackroyd (Dorling Kindersley, 2005)

Mesopotamia: What Life Was Like in Ancient Sumer, Babylon and Assyria (Find Out About) by Lorna Oakes (Southwater, 2004)

Archaeologist
Investigates ancient remains and ruins of buildings in order to find out how people lived in the past.

Curator
Cares for the ancient treasures and collections that are kept in museums and manages the exhibitions.

Diver
Investigates underwater wrecks and archaeological sites such as that of the Colossus of Rhodes or the Pharos at Alexandria.

Egyptologist
An archaeologist who specializes in the study of the buildings and way of life of ancient Egypt.

Visit the Giza pyramids, Cairo, Egypt. Contact: The Egyptian Office of Tourism, Misr Travel Tower, Abbassia Square, Cairo, Egypt Telephone: +20 (0)285 4509/284 1970

To see fabulous treasures from Egypt and ancient Greece, visit:
The British Museum, Great Russell Street, London WC1B 3DG
Tel: +44 (0)20 7323 8299
www.thebritishmuseum.ac.uk

To see wonderful remains from ancient Babylon visit:
Staatliche Museen zu Berlin, Genthinerstra.38D, 10785 Berlin, Germany
Tel: +49 (0)30 266 2987
www.smb.spk-berlin.de

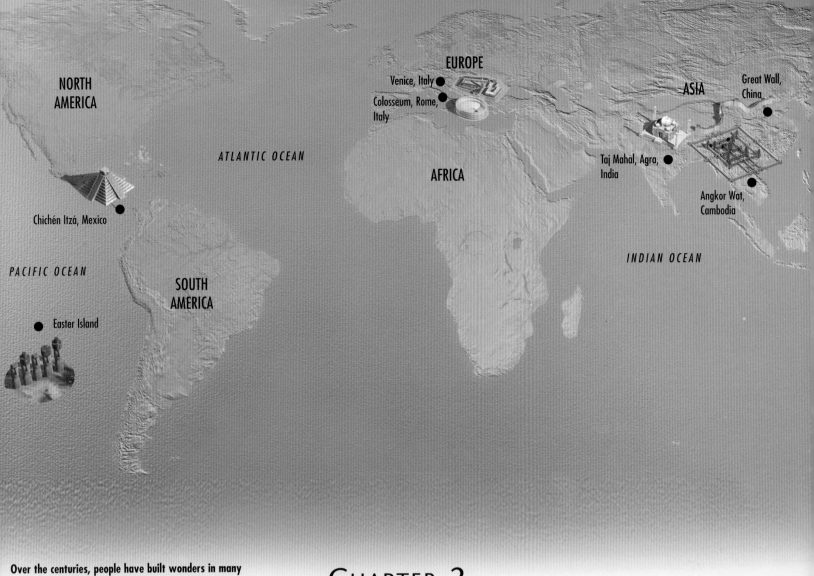

NORTH
AMERICA

ATLANTIC OCEAN

Chichén Itzá, Mexico

PACIFIC OCEAN

SOUTH
AMERICA

Easter Island

EUROPE
Venice, Italy
Colosseum, Rome,
Italy

AFRICA

INDIAN OCEAN

ASIA

Great Wall,
China

Taj Mahal, Agra,
India

Angkor Wat,
Cambodia

**Over the centuries, people have built wonders in many
countries, on different continents, as this map shows.**

CHAPTER 2

The wider world

The ancient wonders of the world did not, of course, include places that were unknown to the ancient Greek geographers. At the time, there were already remarkable sights to be seen in northern Europe, India and China, Africa and the Americas. In medieval Europe, where scholars loved to make numbered lists of everything under the sun, there were constant revisions of the ancient lists. What about prehistoric sites, such as the mysterious stones raised at Stonehenge in southern England in about 2000BCE? And surely the Hagia Sophia, the great Christian church at Constantinople built in 537CE was the wonder of its age? There was no shortage of suggestions, but no definitive list could be made, for it would immediately be overtaken by new marvels – a few of which may be visited on the following pages.

Colosseum at Rome

Imagine a crowd of 50,000 excited people pouring into a huge, oval-shaped building through no fewer than 80 entrances. See them sweltering on the terraces in the heat of the day. Hear the braying trumpets and the vast roar of the crowd which booms and echoes across the city. This is not a modern sports stadium or a rock concert, but Rome in the year 100CE. The building is the Flavian Amphitheatre, known to later generations as the Colosseum.

▼ The cruel 'games' held in Roman amphitheatres were so popular that they were sponsored by many emperors. It was not until 326CE that the games were finally closed down. The great stone blocks of the Flavian Amphitheatre still stand today in the centre of Rome. The visitor today can easily see why the building became known as the Colosseum because of its colossal size.

▼ Rome's Flavian Amphitheatre opened for business in 80CE. It measured 527m around its perimeter and was 57m high. Over the years, it was filled with the very latest technology, allowing the central area to be flooded, or for cages of wild animals to rise up into the arena from the network of rooms below as if by magic. Sailors were employed to rig up canvas awnings as shade for the crowds.

Engineering genius

If the Greeks of 300BCE had been able to see the amazing engineering feats achieved by the Romans four centuries later, they would have had to re-write their lists of world wonders. The four-storey-high Colosseum was spectacular. It could be completely flooded to stage mock naval battles. And the arena could be filled with dazzling white sands – in fact, 'arena' is the Latin word for 'sand'.

▲ Wild beasts were collected from all over the Roman empire and brought to Rome on such a scale that whole regions of the world became stripped of their natural wildlife. When the Colosseum was first opened in 80CE, 5,000 animals were killed in a single day.

Savage 'entertainments'

Other wonders are monuments to humanity's most noble ideals, but the Colosseum was a monument to unspeakable cruelty. The crowds came to this arena to see blood spilt. There were fights between wild animals, with lions encouraged to attack giraffes or camels. There were staged 'hunts', in which people slaughtered vast numbers of wild animals. Sometimes, prisoners would be thrown to the beasts, and the crowd would laugh as they watched them being devoured by tigers or crocodiles.

◀ Gladiators were divided into various classes of combatant. Some fought with short swords and special helmets, others with nets and tridents or with daggers. It was thought at the time that this kind of fighting would educate young Romans, and encourage them to become tough and brave.

The gladiators

One of the most popular spectacles of all those seen in the Colosseum were the fights to the death between gladiators. These were trained fighters, often slaves or ex-prisoners, although some were volunteers. If the crowd believed a gladiator had fought bravely, they might appeal to the patron of the games – perhaps the emperor himself – for the gladiator's life to be spared. If the crowd thought the gladiator had been cowardly, they would demand that he died. Most gladiators had short lives, but successful ones became celebrities and were offered their freedom.

Great Wall of China

The world's longest wall snakes across northern China, crossing mountains and deserts. It stretches from Gansu in the west to the eastern coast. The Chinese call it *wanli changcheng*, the 'Great Wall of Ten Thousand Leagues'. The main wall is about 3,460km long, with an extra 2,860km of branches and spurs. Today, many sections lie in ruins. The best preserved part lies north of the capital, Beijing.

▼ Mongol horsemen, led by the great warrior Temujin, or Genghis Khan ('universal ruler'), rode through the ancient defences of the Great Wall to conquer most of northern China between 1211 and 1223. They went on to rule all China until 1368.

▼ During the 14th and 15th centuries, China was still at constant risk of invasion. This part of the wall was built during this period. Roadways and steps were built along the top of the wall, allowing messengers and soldiers armed with crossbows to travel at speed.

▲ The incredible length of the Great Wall is made clear on this map of China. A network of defences, dating from many different periods of Chinese history, stretches from the Central Asian steppes to the Pacific Ocean. The most visited section of the Great Wall is at Badaling, near Beijing.

Defending the land

From 453 to 221BCE, the Chinese people were divided. They lived in separate kingdoms and their rulers fought endless wars against each other. Some territories were also attacked by fierce raiders from the north, the Xiongnu. Great earthworks were raised to keep these nomadic warriors out of Chinese lands. In 221BCE, Qin Shi Huang, ruler of the Qin kingdom, became the first emperor. He united China and sent soldiers, slaves and peasants to the far north to build new defences. They raised walls of rubble, brick and stone, with strong foundations – the beginnings of the Great Wall.

Rulers and invaders

During the following centuries, the Great Wall was built on and repaired, before parts fell into ruin once again. It provided a useful route for trade, but most rulers discovered that it was inefficient and costly to maintain. In 1215CE, China was overrun by a new enemy from the north, the Mongols, who rode through gaps in the defences. The last great phase of wall-building took place under the Ming emperors, who ruled China from 1368 to 1644.

▲ Watch towers were built at regular intervals along the Great Wall. They were up to 12m tall, and could be used as lookouts or fortresses, housing garrisons of troops and stockpiled supplies. They also served as signal stations, using beacons, smoke or flags for messages, or to warn of invasion.

The greatest wonder

European travellers in China were awestruck by the Great Wall. In the 1660s, Ferdinand Verbiest, a Flemish priest and scientist, reported that 'the Seven Wonders of the World put together are not comparable to this work'. In modern times, the Great Wall has become a symbol of China – its glorious ancient history and its engineering genius.

Angkor Wat

In 1860, a French naturalist called Henri Mouhot was exploring the jungles of Cambodia, in southeast Asia. Underneath a tangle of creepers and tree roots, he discovered an extraordinary group of ancient buildings. Archaeologists began work there and soon uncovered the lost world of the Khmer people.

The past revealed

As the vegetation was stripped away by the archaeologists, the buildings of the medieval Khmer civilization came into view. They belonged to the great capital Angkor Thom, dating back to about 1200CE. A short distance to the south, Mouhot noted the existence of a temple. He described it as greater than 'anything left to us by Greece or Rome'. Angkor Wat (which means 'temple') was less overgrown by the jungle, but it still took many years of hard work to clear it of the surrounding vegetation.

▲ This relief carved in stone from the eastern gallery at Angkor Wat shows a famous image of the Hindu god Vishnu with the god Indra above him. The Angkor Wat temple was dedicated to Vishnu.

▼ Angkor Wat is the most impressive of 100 stone temples surviving around the modern Cambodian town of Siem Reap. In medieval times, there would also have been countless wooden buildings in the area.

▲ A Buddhist monk dressed in saffron-coloured robes meditates at Angkor Wat. The temple was originally a Hindu site, but it has been sacred to the Buddhist faith for over six centuries.

Temple of the five towers

The area that includes the temple of Angkor Wat is the largest religious site on earth, with an area of 163 hectares. The temple had been founded in about 1150 to mark the funeral of Suryavarman II. This king had been the ruler of the Khmer people and a Hindu. He was devoted to the god Vishnu, in whose honour the temple was built and to whom it was dedicated. Angkor Wat's five sandstone towers were created to represent the peaks of Mount Meru, the home of the gods in Hindu mythology. The site was enclosed by a wall 3.6km long, and moated. It has three long, rectangular galleries, one above the other, as well as terraces, and many beautiful statues and reliefs.

Changes in fortune

The impressive temple later became a centre for the Buddhist faith, attracting many pilgrims. However, it was abandoned in the 1430s after attacks on it by the Tai people from the south. About 90 per cent of Cambodians today are of Khmer descent, and Angkor Wat has become a symbol of their ancient culture. The temple's status as a world wonder is confirmed by the visits there of over a million tourists a year. These tourists, however, may well do more damage to the site by simply walking around it than the jungle ever did.

▶ Henri Mouhot's discovery led to the uncovering of many artistic treasures. This serene head is one of those carved on the stone towers of the Bayon, a marvellous temple built at the centre of Angkor Thom by King Jayavarman VII in about 1200. He was a Buddhist and a powerful ruler.

Mysteries of the Pacific

Easter Island, or Rapa Nui, is one of the most remote spots on earth. It lies in the South Pacific Ocean, about 3,600km west of the coast of Chile. Guarding this small island, which is dotted with extinct volcanoes, are gigantic heads of carved stone. Almost a thousand heads gaze over the rolling hills, but their origins are shrouded in mystery.

The seafarers

Between about 1500BCE and 1200CE, the islands of the South Pacific were settled by the Polynesian people, who originated in southeast Asia. These seafarers travelled in canoes with sails, and were skilled navigators. Easter Island was the easternmost point of their travels, and may have been reached, probably from the Marquesas Islands, as early as 400CE. The first Europeans to discover the island were the Dutch, on Easter Sunday in 1722.

▲ A girl in traditional Polynesian costume dances at Ahu Tongariki on Easter Island. This coastal site is in the southeast of the island. It has some of the most massive *moai* of this remote spot. All of them were quarried from the extinct volcano of Rano Raraku. Ahu Tongariki was devastated by a tsunami (a gigantic wave caused by an earthquake) in 1960. The giant heads have since been raised into position once again by archaeologists.

Giant statues

Easter Island's strange statues, called *moai*, were probably carved by the islanders between about 1000 and 1600CE. Some of the *moai*, which have noble faces with curving noses and long earlobes, were arranged in rows on ceremonial stone platforms called *ahu*. And some have *pukau*, cylindrical stone 'topknots', which may originally have been painted dark red. Others have hands with long fingers that rest across the stomach, and many have deep eye-sockets, which archaeologists believe may have been filled with coral.

Figures of power

The statues weigh up to 84 tonnes and some tower more than 11m tall. They probably represented ancestral chiefs and were believed to have great spiritual power. Carving, moving and erecting the *moai* must have been skilled work that took many, many years. Nearly 900 *moai* have been traced so far, some toppled over and others re-erected. About 600 still lie uncompleted, many in the quarry where they were being prepared.

▲ This is the ruin of a typical house at Ahu Tahai, in the east of the island. Its outer stones form the shape of a boat, and would have supported arches made of timber. On the land surrounding their homes, the Easter Islanders grew sweet potatoes, yams, sugar cane and bananas, and they also raised chickens.

◀ The slopes of Rano Raraku are dotted with *moai*, gazing back into an unknown past. The thriving culture of Easter Island rapidly declined after 1600CE. Some historians believe that the islanders cut down too many trees, destroying the environment that supported them. Others think it was because clans fought bitterly for scarce resources. Further disasters struck in the 19th century, when slave traders took away 35 per cent of the island's population to work as labourers or servants in Peru.

Chichén Itzá

The ancient Greeks who drew up the original lists of wonders of the world knew nothing of the Americas. When Europeans finally travelled through Mexico and Peru in the 1500s, they could scarcely believe their eyes. Here were ancient cities, pyramids and temples, as well as great treasuries of gold, silver and jade. A number of peoples were the creators of these great works, particularly the Maya, the Toltecs, the Aztecs and the Incas.

▲ In a game played by the peoples of the region, a rubber ball had to be kept in the air and butted with the body, but it could not be thrown or kicked. It had to pass through this stone ring on the wall.

◀ The game was part of a religious ritual, played in honour of the gods. The ball court at Chichén Itzá was the largest Mayan ball court, measuring 94 by 35 metres.

◀ A stone figure lies on its back, holding a dish. Several of these stone statues, known as *chacmools*, were discovered at Chichén Itzá and elsewhere in the region. They may be associated with human sacrifices that were made to the rain god Chac.

Who built the city?

Many of the most remarkable Mexican sites are on the Yucatán peninsula. This region is flat, hot and very dry, apart from small, sunken lakes called *cenotes*. It was near three of these precious water supplies that a settlement called Chichén Itzá was founded by the Itzá, a Mayan people who had migrated to the region. By 600CE, Chichén Itzá had grown into a city. In about 987, it was probably conquered by a Toltec invader because there is a mixture of Mayan and Toltec-style stonework from this period. After wars among the Maya in the 13th century, the city fell into ruins.

Warriors and skulls

The ruins of Chichén Itzá still stand today. Within an area of 10km², there are temples and terraces, stepped pyramids and stairways, altars, palaces, thrones, inscriptions, market places, ball courts, baths, an observatory and carvings of the gods. The massive Temple of Warriors, bordering the jungle, is surrounded by 60 pillars. Carved in its stone are Toltec warriors with pierced noses, ready to do battle in feathers and headdresses. On the east terrace of the ball court are carved serpents and skulls. The grisly Wall of Skulls was once a place where heads were skewered during human sacrifice.

Ancient civilizations

The ancient peoples of Mexico regarded human sacrifice to the gods as a great honour for the victims. Civilizations such as that of the Maya did not have knowledge of metal tools or the wheel, but they did produce marvellous buildings, jewellery, featherwork, pottery, textiles and wall paintings. They invented calendars and ways of writing, and studied the stars. Spanish soldiers invaded Mexico in 1519, and looted and destroyed many of the wonders they found. However, today the descendants of the Maya still live across a large area of Mexico and Central America.

▲ This pyramid has nine 'steps', representing nine underground worlds, and stands 24 metres high. Its 91 stairs lead to a temple dedicated to Kukulkán. This was not only the supposed name of the Toltec invader, but also of the Plumed Serpent god, also known as Quetzalcoatl. The Spanish called this pyramid the Castillo or castle.

The Taj Mahal

Is this the most beautiful building in the world? The Taj Mahal overlooks the River Yamuna near Agra, in India. It is a mausoleum that was built between 1632 and 1653 by Shah Jahan, the Moghul emperor. The Moghuls were Muslim rulers of much of India at the time. This masterpiece of architecture commemorates the emperor's wife, known as Mumtaz Mahal.

▲ Shah Jahan was born in Lahore (now in Pakistan) in 1592. In 1612, he married Arjumand Bann Begum, who was famed for her beauty. He had a number of wives, but she was his favourite. She took the name Mumtaz Mahal, meaning 'adornment of the palace', and bore him 14 children, seven of which survived childhood.

Marble and gemstones

The Moghul emperors encouraged the creation of beautiful art and architecture. After Mumtaz Mahal died in 1631, Shah Jahan raised a workforce of over 20,000 skilled men. The finest white marble was quarried and precious stones – amethysts, jade, lapis lazuli, turquoise, coral and mother-of-pearl – were imported from all over Asia to decorate the building. The precious stones were inlaid into the stonework in beautiful flower patterns. As the central building rose, towering arches appeared, designed in the Persian style. Verses from the Islamic scriptures, the *Quran*, adorned the walls in a flowing Arabic script.

▲ The tiles and inlays that decorate the Taj Mahal show Indian and Persian influences. The style is elaborate but subtle, so that it does not distract the eye from the building as a whole.

Building paradise

Mumtaz Mahal was more than a wife and mother. She was also Shah Jahan's closest friend and political adviser. When she died, it is said he refused food for eight days. To reflect his devotion to her, he wanted to build the most beautiful monument. The Taj Mahal was topped with four canopies and a vast, gleaming white dome. Four soaring minarets, or prayer towers, flanked the tomb, and there was also a mosque and courtyards. The complex was set in a large formal Moghul garden divided into four parts, which included pools that reflected the image of the main building. The Taj Mahal was a monument to God, and to human love and grief. However, it also served to show off the power and wealth of Shah Jahan, although the expense of building it nearly bankrupted the Moghul empire.

◄ The beautiful stonework of the Taj Mahal has been threatened in modern times by air pollution from factories and city traffic, and by the many tourists who visit the site.

The final days

It is said that Shah Jahan planned to build a matching mausoleum for himself, in black stone. However, his plans were not realized. He became ill in 1658 and his four sons rebelled against him. One of them, Aurangzeb, gained control of the empire and, to cement his power, imprisoned his father in Agra Fort. Tended by Jahanara, his eldest daughter, Shah Jahan died there eight years later, in 1666, and was finally buried in the Taj Mahal next to Mumtaz Mahal. Today, the Taj Mahal is the best-known image of India, shown in countless photographs gleaming in the moonlight or lit up by the dawn.

▼ Two Hindu women celebrate the festival of Diwali beside the pools of the Taj Mahal. Hindus, Muslims and people of all faiths are equally inspired by this sublime building.

Canals of Venice

The cities of Europe have produced many wonders in the last 1,000 years. There are soaring medieval cathedrals with beautiful coloured stained glass windows, mighty castle towers and strong city walls, as well as lavish palaces which contain skilful paintings and tapestries by the most talented artists. One of the most inspiring cities of all is Venice, in Italy, with its canals and waterways instead of roads. It is a city built on a group of low-lying islands, and it seems to the visitor that it has risen directly from the sea.

▲ Central Venice is made up of 118 little islands, joined together by about 400 bridges. Between them are a maze of waterways and canals. This aerial photograph shows the great loop of the Grand Canal in the heart of the city. This breathtaking city has been built in a very watery location.

The town built on water

In ancient times, the coast around Venice was marshy. A shallow lagoon was protected from the open sea by little islands and sandbanks. Refugees from the mainland settled here in the 5th century CE, when Italy was being repeatedly invaded. Surprisingly, the refugees prospered. They collected salt, they fished, they built ships and they made glass. Above all, they traded. In the Middle Ages, merchants from Venice had control over the trade with Asia, importing precious silks and spices. To build the foundations for a new city, they sank millions of timber poles into the soggy ground.

A life on the water

By the 15th century, Venice had become one of the richest cities in the world. At its peak, it had 36,000 sailors moving more than 3,000 ships in and out of its harbour. During the following centuries, splendid bridges, markets, boatyards, palaces and churches were built. However, there were few roads. Venetians preferred to travel by boat, along a network of beautiful canals. Venice was a significant port. The Venetians knew they depended on the sea, and each year confirmed this in a public ceremony. The leader of the city, or Doge, was rowed out to sea in a golden galley. He threw a ring into the waves, making the declaration that the city was wedded to the sea.

The 'most serene' city

Venice began to decline as a political power at the end of the 18th century. However, it remained a centre of art, music and theatre, with an elegant carnival that is still held every year. Venice became famous as *La Serenissima*, the 'most serene' of cities. It still attracts countless visitors. No one can ever forget the sight of the city skyline appearing for the first time above the pale blue waters of the lagoon, or the streets that are made of water. However, Venice's future is under threat. Sea levels are rising and floods there are becoming more common. It is a fragile city, requiring many difficult planning decisions if its precious buildings and treasures are to be saved.

▼ At street level, it is all water, so the easiest way to travel is by boat. Today, motorboats and water buses called *vaporeti* ply many of the canals, but for many tourists the only way to travel is by gondola (below). This is the traditional, black-painted boat of the canals, with a narrow hull nearly 11m long, and an upturned prow and stern. The gondola is propelled by a gondolier holding a long oar.

▶ A flood flows down the Piazetta into St Mark's Square in the centre of Venice, stranding the chairs and tables that are normally occupied by tourists. The grand building is the Doge's Palace, the medieval centre of government. The architecture shows influences of both Asia and Europe, a reminder of the city's trading heritage. Venice is used to flooding, but there are grave concerns for the future safety of the city.

SUMMARY OF CHAPTER 2: THE WIDER WORLD

There are about 1,000 gigantic stone heads on Easter Island in the southern Pacific.

Rome and beyond
The ancient Greeks were only familiar with southern Europe, western Asia and northern Africa. Beyond the limits of their world were distant, unknown lands, all with their own mysteries and wonders. By 2,000 years ago, Roman power was expanding and Roman engineers were building roads, aqueducts and great cities. The **Colosseum** in Rome was opened in 80CE. It was a considerable architectural achievement.

The world opens up
For the 1,200 years after the collapse of the Roman empire in 476CE, beautiful buildings and monuments were created on almost every continent. These became more widely known as a great age of world exploration began in the 14th and 15th centuries. Moroccans and Venetians travelled to China, Chinese traders travelled to Arabia and east Africa and European sailors reached the Americas.

From China to Mexico
The most impressive Chinese monument is the **Great Wall**, built over many centuries to keep out invaders. One of the world's biggest religious sites is the magnificent **Angkor Wat**, in Cambodia, constructed in about 1150. The most mysterious of all world wonders are the gigantic stone heads raised on remote **Easter Island**, in the Pacific Ocean, from 1000 to 1600. Before the European discovery of the Americas in 1492, the Maya, Toltecs, Aztecs and Incas were building great cities and temples. **Chichén Itzá** in Mexico thrived from 600 to 1200.

Grace and beauty
The most beautiful of the later world wonders is surely the **Taj Mahal**, a mausoleum built by the Moghul emperor of India for his wife, finished in 1652. Europe's great cities – Paris, Florence and London – are full of treasures. One of the most perfect cities is **Venice**, erected on low-lying islands in an Italian lagoon – truly a city built on water.

Go further...

Read more about the amazing wonders of the wider world:
www.metmuseum.org/toah/hd/eais/hd_eais.htm
www.venetia.it
www.mysteriousplaces.com/mayan/TourEntrance.html

The Great Wall of China: Great Structures in History by Rachel Lynette (KidHaven Press, 2004)

The Taj Mahal: Great Buildings by Christine Moorcroft (Steck-Vaughn, 1997)

Secrets in Stone: All About Maya Hieroglyphs by Laurie Coulter, Sarah Jane English (Madison Press, 2001)

Anthropologist
Studies the development of human cultures, customs and beliefs.

Art historian
Studies old pictures, carvings, designs and sculptures.

Conservationist
Looks after old buildings and sites keeping them in good repair and protecting them.

Sinologist
Studies the history, culture and languages of China.

Stonemason
Cuts, carves and finishes stone used in buildings and restorations.

Explore the site of the Colosseum, battleground of the gladiators, and then visit Rome itself:
www.the-colosseum.net/idx-en.htm

Find out about the temple of Angkor Wat and other endangered sites on the History Channel site:
www.history.com/classroom/unesco/angkor/index2.html

Discover more about Chichén Itzá and other Central American wonders:
www.mnsu.edu/emuseum/archaeology/sites/meso_america/chichenitza.html

There is a great site about oriental architecture and the Taj Mahal at:
www.orientalarchitecture.com/agra/tajmahalindex.htm

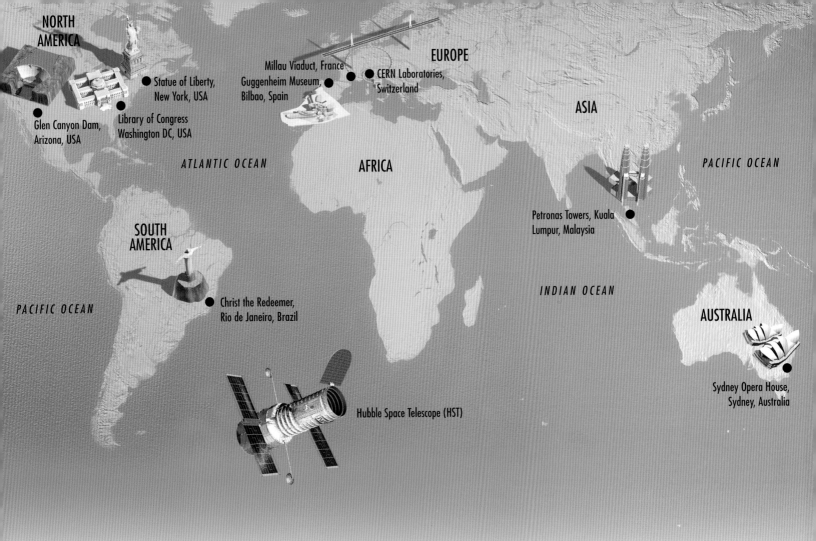

NORTH AMERICA

● Statue of Liberty, New York, USA

● Glen Canyon Dam, Arizona, USA

● Library of Congress Washington DC, USA

ATLANTIC OCEAN

SOUTH AMERICA

PACIFIC OCEAN

● Christ the Redeemer, Rio de Janeiro, Brazil

Millau Viaduct, France
Guggenheim Museum, Bilbao, Spain

EUROPE

● CERN Laboratories, Switzerland

AFRICA

ASIA

PACIFIC OCEAN

INDIAN OCEAN

Petronas Towers, Kuala Lumpur, Malaysia ●

AUSTRALIA

● Sydney Opera House, Sydney, Australia

Hubble Space Telescope (HST)

Some of the modern wonders are now not earthbound or even wonders that we can see. Satellite technology and the World Wide Web have transformed people's lives.

CHAPTER 3

Modern wonders

In the 18th and 19th centuries, Europe and North America saw a rush of scientific and technical advances – the Industrial Revolution. There were brilliant inventions such as steamships, trains and cars. In the 20th century, newer styles of building were designed, using concrete, steel and glass. Soaring skyscrapers took over cities. By the 21st century, many of humanity's ancient dreams had come true. People could fly and travel in space, they could build incredible dams and bridges. The United States Library of Congress could house more than 29 million books. The World Wide Web could provide access to almost unlimited information around the globe. Space telescopes could see to the ends of the Universe. Which of these marvels will be rated as lasting wonders only future generations will tell.

Top of the world!

The urge to build tall is an ancient one. The Pharos of Alexandria was just one of several very early attempts at high-rise architecture, as people sought to emphasize their power and status. However, it was not until the 19th century that the invention of new building materials made the building of modern 'skyscrapers' possible. The new towers relied on the use of extremely strong iron and steel, as well as tough plate glass, rather than on brick or stone.

The first skyscrapers

In 1871, a terrible fire destroyed the city of Chicago in the United States. It had to be completely rebuilt in the following years, at a time when high-quality steel was becoming cheaper. New metal-framed skyscrapers began to soar upwards. The strength of iron was demonstrated by the French engineer Gustave Eiffel, whose Eiffel Tower in Paris became the highest structure in the world in 1889. Skyscrapers, like the ancient wonders of the world, were designed to impress and show off wealth and status. New inventions, such as the rapid 'elevator', or lift, made tall buildings more practical to use.

American dreams

New York City soon took the lead in high-rise building. Confined to the island of Manhattan, the city could only build upwards rather than outwards. In 1930, the elegant, spired Chrysler Building rose 319m. It was outdone just one year later by one of the most famous skyscrapers of all time, the Empire State Building (381m). The 415m-high twin towers of the World Trade Center dominated the New York skyline from 1973 until 2001, when they were tragically destroyed in a terrorist attack. Chicago had regained the lead in 1974 with the Sears Tower – a dizzying 442m high.

▶ These construction workers are taking a lunch break on an exposed steel beam, some 245m above the ground! They do not wear safety harnesses or hard hats. The year is 1932 and they are working on the 266m-high RCA Building, in New York's Rockefeller Center. The skyscraper is known today as the General Electric (GE) Building.

◀ Today, each new skyscraper sensation is soon overtaken by another, as every city around the world competes. The Petronas Towers (452m) in Kuala Lumpur, Malaysia, held the record from 1998 to 2004.

Concrete and steel

Skyscraper design brought in a whole new range of building methods. Concrete was 'reinforced' with steel rods. Huge rafts of concrete could be laid down as support for the foundations, or tough piles drilled deep down into rock. Buildings were assembled around a central core. Planning on such a scale was a difficult job, and carried with it all kinds of environmental concerns. Projects needed computer modelling and even, like aircraft, testing in wind tunnels. New materials mean that recent skyscrapers have all sorts of incredible shapes and finishes.

321m – Eiffel Tower, Paris, France (1889)

381m – Empire State Building, New York, USA (1931)

452m – Petronas Towers, Kuala Lumpur, Malaysia (1998)

509m – Taipei 101, Taiwan (2003)

553m – CN Tower, Toronto, Canada (1976)

? – Burj Dubai, UAE (unfinished)

▲ The height of skyscrapers, and also of free-standing structures such as broadcasting towers, has continued to rise at a bewildering rate for over a century. In 1931, the Empire State Building was over twice the height of the Singer Building, which had astounded New Yorkers only 23 years earlier. By 2003, the pagoda-like Taipei 101 in Taiwan had reached the dizzying height of 509m, and it had to be specially protected against earthquakes and tropical storms. Its lifts can whisk people up to the viewing station on the 89th floor at a speed of 63km/h. The Burj Dubai, under construction since 2005, is expected to be a great deal higher even than the Taipei 101. All are extraordinary feats of engineering, but it remains to be seen which ones capture the public imagination and qualify as wonders of the world.

Architecture and the arts

In the last 100 years, architects around the world have created incredible new cities, with public buildings that inspire and provoke the imagination. Some of these are concert halls or art galleries; others are offices or libraries. They have been given form by exciting new technologies, including computer modelling, and the creation of amazing new materials such as plastics, plate glass, steel and reinforced concrete.

A temple of the arts

Bilbao is the chief city of the Basque country, a region of Europe that extends from Spain into France. The Basque way of life has very ancient roots, but the newest addition to the architecture of Bilbao is a vision of the future. It is the Guggenheim Museum of Modern Art, which opened in 1997. The designer was an American, Frank Gehry, and the building's extraordinary curves and shapes were inspired by the lines of a ship.

◀ The roof of Sydney Opera House has more than a million tiles made of dazzling white granite, set in smooth-surfaced panels. The tiles are glazed, which helps to keep them clean, but occasionally they need to be repaired or replaced.

Shells by the harbour

Another modern building, on the other side of the world, is generally recognized as a new wonder. Just as ancient Greeks travelled to see the Great Pyramid in Egypt, so tourists now flock to Australia to see this famous landmark, and new brides fly from as far away as Japan to be photographed against its skyline. The Sydney Opera House is built on Bennelong Point in the city of Sydney, close to another famous landmark, Sydney Harbour Bridge. The Opera House's ten roofs are shaped like giant sea shells, or perhaps more like the billowing sails of the yachts that cross the blue waters of the harbour below.

◀ Bilbao's Guggenheim Museum rises magnificently from the River Nervión. It was made possible by computer modelling, which explored the possibilities and limits of structures, stresses, shapes and materials. The museum is built of limestone, covered with plates of titanium like fish-scales, and sheathed in glass.

▶ Many technological problems had to be overcome during the building of Sydney Opera House. Public arguments over the design became very heated. Most people now agree that this is one of the landmark buildings of modern times.

A building to remember

The Sydney Opera House was designed by Danish architect Jørn Utzøn, and built between 1958 and 1973. The building complex covers an area of 1.8 hectares and is supported by 580 concrete piers, sunk deep underground. Inside, there are more than 1,000 rooms, including theatres, studios and concert halls. These are used for opera, dance, theatre and all kinds of musical performances. The main concert hall can seat more than 2,500 people.

Water wonders

Water is essential for our survival on Earth. It allows people to drink, to irrigate crops, to use ships and to generate power. Water can also pose a threat to life, for example when the sea floods the land, or rivers break their banks. The people who harness the power of water, or build defences against flooding, have produced some of the most superlative feats of engineering in modern times all around the world. Sometimes in very dangerous conditions and with great loss of life, they have built canals, irrigation systems, dams and flood barriers.

▲ The cascade of more than 62,000 cubic metres of water per second, thundering down the spillway of the Itaipu Dam, is an incredible sight. This truly massive hydroelectric scheme opened in 1984 on the borders of Brazil and Paraguay. Its turbines produce more electricity than ten nuclear power stations.

◄ Tugs tow a ship through the Panama Canal in its early days. Thousands of labourers died building this waterway between 1880 and its opening in 1914. It was one of the largest, and most difficult, engineering projects ever undertaken. Today, more than 14,000 ships a year pass through the canal. In 2006, plans were announced for a major new upgrade, allowing more and bigger ships to pass through.

The great canals
Humans have been building canals for at least 6,000 years. Many of these should be ranked as world wonders, including China's Grand Canal, completed in 1327. It is 1,781km long and at one point employed five million labourers. The Suez Canal between the Red Sea and the Mediterranean Sea opened in 1869, allowing big ships to bypass the whole continent of Africa in their travels from east to west or vice versa. The year 1914 saw the opening of the Panama Canal in Central America, begun by the French, and finished by the Americans. This waterway links the Atlantic and Pacific Oceans, and allows ships to avoid having to travel right round the tip of South America.

Dramatic dams

The 20th century was the great age of dam-building. The Grand Coulee Dam (1942) in Washington State, USA, was built with more than 80 million cubic metres of concrete. The Aswan High Dam in Egypt, completed in 1970, contained 17 times as much rock as the pyramids at Giza. The Rogun Dam (1990) in Tajikistan in Central Asia, soars to the height of 335m. The most incredible project of all is China's Three Gorges Dam which should be operational by 2009. This will be the world's biggest generator of hydroelectric power and will also control floods on the Chang Jiang, the world's third longest river.

Building for the future

Giant dams are mind-boggling wonders of the modern world, but they often cause real hardship – over a million people have already been displaced from their homes by the Three Gorges Dam. Dams are also sometimes disastrous for the environment. Perhaps engineering that will have the most lasting value will be schemes that protect people from rising sea levels. The world's biggest flood defences are the Delta scheme, an ongoing effort to prevent the waterlogged Dutch coast being drowned by the North Sea. Since 1986, this amazing project has sealed off four major rivers with dams and barriers.

◀ This is the Glen Canyon hydroelectric power scheme, which dams the Colorado River in Arizona, in the United States. Its rim curves around for an amazing 476m, and the base of its wall is 91m thick. Opened in 1966, it is the perfect example of the strength and beauty of modern dams. However, like many dams, Glen Canyon has also been much criticised for its impact on the environment and on the natural flow of the great river that feeds it.

Building bridges

Bridges are structures that often combine great beauty with phenomenal strength. Some bridges are supported by curved arches, while others (beam bridges) are flat and rigid, supported by tall pillars (piers). Suspension bridges support the roadway (deck) with thick steel cables, slung from high towers. Many of these are wonders of the modern age.

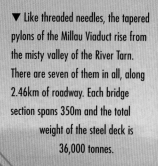

▼ Like threaded needles, the tapered pylons of the Millau Viaduct rise from the misty valley of the River Tarn. There are seven of them in all, along 2.46km of roadway. Each bridge section spans 350m and the total weight of the steel deck is 36,000 tonnes.

◀ Bridge-building is a fine art. This is the Tsing Ma Suspension Bridge in Hong Kong, China. Its 1,377m-long deck carries both road and rail. It is supported by steel cables that are suspended from two 206m-high towers and anchored in deep concrete at both ends of the bridge. The cables are spun over high iron saddles on top of each tower. Each main cable on the bridge is more than a metre thick and made up of 70,000 strands.

Tallest road bridge in the world

The Millau Viaduct opened in 2004. It carries traffic across the wide valley of the River Tarn, in southern France. The viaduct is a type of beam bridge, and its roadway rests on piers that extend upwards as tall pylons. The deck is cable-stayed, which means that it is also held firm by powerful cables which fan out from the bridge's pylons. The biggest pylon soars to a height of 343m, making the Millau Viaduct the world's tallest road bridge. The road passes 267m above the Tarn, an altitude exceeded only by the 321m-high Royal Gorge Bridge in the Rocky Mountains of Colorado in the United States.

Famous bridges around the world

Many bridges are candidates for the title of modern wonder. One of the bridge systems that crosses Lake Pontchartain in the United States (1969) is more than 38km long. The Akashi-Kaikyo Suspension Bridge in Japan has a single span of nearly 2km and a total length of more than 3.9km. However, it is not always the highest or the longest bridges that are the best known or most loved by the public. The ornate Tower Bridge (1894), which can raise its deck to allow ships to pass through, has become a symbol of the city of London. In the United States, the graceful Golden Gate Bridge (1937) is internationally famous as an emblem of San Francisco.

Creating a wonder

Planning a grand bridge like the Millau Viaduct is an arduous task. Before it was built, various routes had to be considered. Which would cause the least disruption to the town of Millau? Which would be the least expensive to build? Which was the shortest route? Which would cause the least pollution and environmental damage? The combination of design, engineering and architecture used to build this bridge was an international effort, involving the French, the British and the Dutch. The final project took three years to build and employed 520 workers. It also employed electronic labour, for the mechanics of the construction were carefully controlled by computer.

▲ This is CERN, headquarters of the multi-national European Organization for Nuclear Research, founded in 1959. It was scientists here who devised the amazing World Wide Web in the 1990s. By coincidence, this place is also a wonder of the world in its own right. Located on the French-Swiss border, it includes an underground tunnel that forms a circle 27km long (indicated by the white line in this picture). This tunnel is used to research the nature of matter and nuclear particles.

The computer age

The first computers were developed in North America and Europe in the 1940s and 1950s. They were hulking monsters, with large cables but little brain power. They were only found in offices or universities. After the invention of the microchip, or integrated circuit, in 1958 and microprocessors in 1971, computers became smaller and smaller, but ever more powerful. These changes led to the development of the first personal computers in the 1980s. People could now have the equivalent of several Alexandrian libraries in their own home or office or laboratory. The computer revolution had completely changed the ways in which people lived and worked.

▶ Computer services are already interacting or merging with all sorts of other communications media such as telephones, radios, televisions, newspapers, CDs and DVDs. The electronic world created in these ways is sometimes called cyberspace. It is an imaginary world and yet it has a practical impact on everyday life. Today, most businesses, schools, hospitals and governments are dependent on computers. Cyberspace is rather like an extension of the human mind, for the computer too must arrange, classify, store and process information.

Info lab

Ever since humans first learned to write and record information, they have built centres where data could be stored and communicated. Around 4,000 years ago, the palace of Ebla (today's Tell Mardikh in Syria) was one such place. Records kept there were written on many thousands of clay tablets and stored on shelves. The next centre devised to house information technology was the library. One very famous library founded by Ptolemy II at Alexandria, Egypt, in the 3rd century BCE, could store hundreds of thousands of manuscripts. Today, the biggest information and communication centre the world has ever known is available in your own sitting-room. Its twin 'wonders' are the Internet and the World Wide Web.

Networks and webs

In 1983, universities in the United States began to link up computer networks to aid communications. Other networks also began to connect and this was the origin of the Internet, a global conglomeration made up of millions of networks. It could be used to carry e-mails and many other kinds of communications.

The most amazing information system using the Internet was to be the World Wide Web. This was developed in the early 1990s by English computer scientist Tim Berners-Lee and a group of other scientists at the nuclear physics research centre, CERN, in Europe. They developed ways of linking documents using a language called hypertext. They also invented a whole system of websites, browsers and search engines.

In cyberspace

The computer was now no longer just a means of storing data. It was a powerful research tool which, like the human brain, could follow up associations and connections. It could access a newspaper in Japan, a library in Australia or a shop in Italy, all in a matter of seconds. The traditional wonders of the world were real places or objects that one could visit, walk around and touch. This new wonder had created a virtual world of its own, in cyberspace.

▼ Real libraries are still very necessary in the age of the World Wide Web. The fine old library below is at Trinity College, Dublin, in Ireland. It has about four million books, many of which are very rare. The biggest modern library is the United States Library of Congress in Washington DC. It has 853km of shelving, more than 29 million books, 2.7 million recordings, 12 million photographs, 4.8 million maps and 58 million manuscripts. That certainly qualifies it as another wonder of the world.

Modern colossi

The Colossus of Rhodes may have disappeared long ago, but people are still fascinated and inspired by gigantic statues. Today's colossi often represent religious figures, such as Jesus Christ or the Buddha, or sometimes national heroes or political leaders. One massive female figure, at Volgograd in Russia, commemorates the Battle of Stalingrad, fought in 1942–43. The statue was designed in 1967 and built in concrete and steel. It is 82.3m high and weighs over 8,000 tonnes.

Christ the Redeemer

A statue of Jesus Christ with outstretched arms rises high above the city of Rio de Janeiro in Brazil. Completed in 1931, it is 38m tall and built of reinforced concrete faced with weather-resistant soapstone. The statue stands on a 710m-high peak, Corcovado, on the outskirts of the city. The added height of the mountain makes this modern colossus the ultimate city landmark.

▼ Like any true wonder of the world, the 1,145-tonne statue of Christ the Redeemer that towers over Rio de Janeiro has become the emblem of the city and of the whole country of Brazil. Its open arms, with a span of 30m, seem to embrace the world. Tourists can reach the base of the statue by road, rack-and-pinion railway or hiking trail. The view over the sprawling city, the sparkling sea, and distant hills and mountain peaks is spectacular.

A symbol of liberty

With its crown of rays, its upheld torch and its position at the approaches to the harbour of New York City, the statue of 'Liberty Enlightening the World' is clearly inspired by the ancient Colossus of Rhodes. The statue was inaugurated in 1886. Before the days of air travel, the Statue of Liberty was often the first thing that European immigrants and tourists travelling by ship saw as they approached the United States. The statue was a gift from the French people and was designed by the French sculptor Frédéric Auguste Bartholdi.

Story of a statue

To put Liberty in place needed a feat of engineering, and the engineer who arranged it was Gustave Eiffel, who also built the famous Eiffel Tower in Paris. The Statue of Liberty was shaped from copper sheets bolted to an iron framework. It was assembled in France between 1874 and 1884, shipped in pieces across the Atlantic Ocean and erected on a small island in New York harbour. The statue stands 93m high, including the stone pedestal. Inside, there are stairways leading to the torch and a viewing platform in the crown.

▼ The raised torch on the Statue of Liberty symbolizes the spirit of freedom, a spirit shown by the people of America in the American Revolution of 1775–83. This war saw the Americans break away from British rule to found the United States. The rays in the statue's crown represent the seven oceans and seven continents. The monument is one of the most famous standing in the world today.

Reaching other worlds

The people who built the world's first wonders were fascinated by the sky at night. They built monuments that towered to the heavens. They built observatories to study the movements of planets and stars. In the 17th century CE, scientists began to use telescopes to study the sky more closely. In the 21st century, we can launch giant telescopes, such as the Hubble Space Telescope and the James Webb Space Telescope, to orbit our planet and scan the mysteries of deepest space.

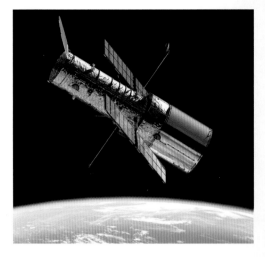

▲ The Hubble Space Telescope is a telescope that images rays of light. Its perfectly smooth main mirror measures 2.4m across. More than 13m long and weighing 11 tonnes, the spacecraft is powered by arrays of solar panels, which convert the sun's rays into electricity. HST is now nearing the end of its life.

The Hubble Space Telescope investigates

In 1990, a new observatory was launched into orbit around Earth. It was named after the great American astronomer Edwin P. Hubble (1889–1953). The Hubble Space Telescope (HST) was programmed to circle the planet every 97 minutes. Doing this at a height of 575km above the Earth's surface, the HST was clear of the distorting effects of gases in the Earth's atmosphere. At first, the telescope had some problems, but these were fixed by Space Shuttle missions which linked up with the HST. Soon the observatory was sending back to Earth breathtaking images of space. Incredibly, HST has shown us new galaxies being born that are so far away that their light has taken 13.7 billion years to reach us. We are looking back almost to the origins of the Universe itself.

A new space wonder

The United States National Aeronautics and Space Administration (NASA) plans to replace the Hubble Space Telescope with a new telescope that images chiefly infrared rays, which have a longer wavelength than light. The new telescope will have a mirror that is 6.5m in diameter. The James Webb Space Telescope (JWST) is scheduled to be launched in 2013, and will operate some 1.5 million kilometres from its home planet. It will take three months to reach this distant orbit. JWST should be able to see back even further than Hubble, giving us valuable information about how the Universe was formed.

Other wonders, other worlds

Space telescopes are supported by all kinds of advanced telescopes and observatories back on Earth. Many scan the skies to pick up radio waves, which have longer wavelengths than infrared. Russia's RATAN 600 radio telescope is the world's biggest, with an antenna which is 576m in diameter. The United States' Very Large Array (VLA) is made up of 27 units linked in a gigantic Y formation. Each unit has a 25m-long antenna. Spacecraft will continue to probe the secrets of space in the centuries to come – maybe they will discover wonders of which we can scarcely dream.

▶ The Hubble Space Telescope has sent back to Earth hundreds of thousands of spectacular images from space. It imaged M16, known as the 'Eagle Nebula', in 2004. This nebula is a vast cloud of cold hydrogen and dust, and is a breeding-ground for new stars. The towering column seen here is believed to have a height of about 90 trillion kilometres.

◀ This is the incredible new space observatory, the James Webb Space Telescope (JWST). Its mission will be to seek images of the earliest galaxies being formed, to discover more about the formation of stars and planetary systems, and to analyze planets to see if they are capable of supporting life.

SUMMARY OF CHAPTER 3: MODERN WONDERS

The Statue of Liberty in New York harbour is truly a modern colossus.

Science and progress

The Industrial Age led to rapid changes in technology and the creation of new materials with many different applications, such as plastics. In the 20th century, new world wonders followed each other in quick succession and most now served a useful purpose. People believed that science would set humanity on a course of steady progress.

Modern magic

By the 21st century, some of that faith in science and technology had been eroded. Many inventions had polluted the planet and used up its precious resources. Wars and famines had shown that nightmares could come true as well as dreams. Even so, the marvels of the 21st century would have seemed to be pure magic to our ancestors. What would an ancient Greek poet have made of a laptop computer connected to the Internet?

New buildings

Where should we look for modern wonders of the world? Four of the seven ancient wonders were buildings, and modern architecture offers many options. Skyscraper mania began in the 1880s – the **Taipei 101** (2003) is currently tallest at 509 metres, but is scheduled to be outstripped by the **Burj Dubai** project. The most exciting modern architecture often belongs to public buildings, including the **Sydney Opera House** (1973) in Australia or the **Guggenheim Museum** (1997) in Bilbao, Spain.

Reaching for the stars

The last 50 years have seen astonishing advances in the building of dams and bridges. Recent examples such as the **Millau Viaduct** are wonders of civil engineering, but massive dams such as the **Three Gorges** in China may have a serious impact on the environment. The monuments perhaps closest in spirit to the ancient wonders of the world are modern colossi, such as **Christ the Redeemer** (1931) in Rio de Janeiro, Brazil. However, today perhaps the most incredible of all the wonders are the **World Wide Web** and the **spacecraft** that explore new worlds.

Go further...

There is no shortage of suggestions for modern wonders of the world:
http://ce.eng.usf.edu/ pharos/wonders/pharos.html
http://wonderclub.com/WorldWonders /ModernWonders.html
www.asce.org/history/seven_ wonders.cfm
www.travelersdigest.com/seven_ modern_wonders.htm

Sky Boys: How They Built the Empire State Building by Deborah Hopkinson and James E. Ransome (Schwartz & Wade Books, 2006)

The Sydney Opera House, Building World Landmarks by Peggy J. Parks (Blackbirch Press, 2004)

Architect
Designs, plans and supervises buildings of all kinds.

Astronomer
Studies stars, planets and other space phenomena.

Civil engineer
Designs, plans and supervises the structure of bridges, dams and tunnels.

Construction worker
Builds buildings of all sorts, working with different materials and machines.

Discover more about modern wonders of the world and make up your own list:
http://worldvstore.com/ modernwonders.htm

Find out about the largest waterways, biggest dams and longest bridges of the modern world:
www.guinnessworldrecords.com

Discover all there is to know about tall buildings on the exhibition site at:
www.moma.org/tallbuildings

Find out what you can do to help UNESCO's World Heritage organization care for wonders of the world:
http://whc.unesco.org

World heritage

The world has more than seven wonders. Indeed, it has more than seven hundred wonders. These great buildings, monuments and works of engineering represent more than part of our history. They are our heritage, something to be cared for and preserved so that they can be passed down from generation to generation.

The Imperial Palace, Beijing, China (1420)

Why care?

Why do wonders of the world matter? Many are ancient ruins already, and others – however beautiful or interesting – simply hold up modern development in our cities. Surely we should be more concerned with the present, rather than obsessed with how lives were lived in the past?

The fact is that these sites remain an inspiration. They show us not only what humans have achieved in the past, but what they are capable of creating in the future. They demonstrate arts, crafts, engineering skills, cooperation and imagination, as well as a natural curiosity about human existence. Of course, many wonders also show the darker side of human nature. Medieval castles may look picturesque, but they were originally designed as centres from which kings and lords carried out warfare and oppression. However, there are also lessons to be learned from these monuments.

Under threat

Many heritage sites are endangered and the threats to their survival are many and varied. Some sites are at risk because over the centuries time and the weather have eroded them – perhaps timbers have rotted or foundations subsided. Many sites suffer damage from earthquakes or warfare. In recent years, rainfall has often become polluted by fumes from traffic exhaust or industrial emissions. This 'acid rain' can eat away particularly at ancient stone. Another threat comes from the development of cities. A palace or temple may be dwarfed by new skyscrapers and hidden from view. Even when a site has been well preserved, it may suffer from the thousands of visitors who swarm over it day after day.

Conserving heritage sites

Around the world, local and national organizations care for conservation and restoration. The United Nations Educational, Scientific and Cultural Organization (UNESCO) registers world heritage sites. It oversees the conservation of such sites and provides emergency funding when necessary.

Rock-hewn chuches, Lalibela, Ethiopia (10th to 13th centuries)

Central and eastern Europe
Central Europe has a rich history, and in Poland, the sites are very varied, for example the grim castle of the medieval Teutonic knights at Malbork and the magnificent old city centre of Krakow in the south. Two beautiful and historic cities are Prague, capital of the Czech Republic, and Budapest, capital of Hungary. Eastern Europe includes the splendours of Russia, as can be seen in the city of St Petersburg. The heart of Moscow, the Russian capital, is dominated by the red walls and the glittering domed churches within the Kremlin, the centre of government.

Europe – west, north and south
Conservation problems in Europe include pollution, urban development and mass tourism. Even so, Western Europe has some of the best conserved heritage sites in the world. There are prehistoric monuments such as 4,000-year-old Stonehenge in England or the Altamira Caves in Spain. There are the magnificent remains of ancient Greece, such as the Parthenon (447–432BCE), the temple of the goddess Athena that towers over Athens. The mark of ancient Rome is everywhere. The triple-decker, 49m-high Pont du Gard in southern France is a combined viaduct and aqueduct, built by the Romans around 150CE.

The Parthenon (447–432BCE) on the Acropolis in Athens, Greece

Medieval Europe produced spectacular cathedrals such as Chartres in France (1220) and Ulm in Germany (started 1337), the world's tallest church with a 161.5m-high spire.

The cathedral of Notre Dame de Paris (1160–1345), on the Île de la Cité in the heart of France's capital city

Great castles were built right across Europe. The Alhambra in Granada is a breathtaking fortification and Islamic palace, built in the days when the Moors ruled Spain.

Italy saw a great surge of creativity in the 15th and 16th centuries. This Renaissance, or 'rebirth', resulted in the building of elegant cities such as Florence and Siena. In northern Europe, in the Low Countries (now the Netherlands and Belgium) and also in Scandinavia, merchants built their houses along busy canals or waterfronts so that they could import and export goods. The Industrial Revolution began in the British Isles, and here the heritage of the 18th and 19th centuries has its own beauty – docks, tin mines, textile mills, potteries and ironworks. Soon this industrial world would sprawl across northern Europe – and the northeastern United States.

Northern Africa

The extraordinary monuments of Egypt, such as the tombs of the Valley of the Kings, are known around the world. The massive statues at Abu Simbel, more than 3,200 years old, had to be rescued and moved from the dangers of the rising waters of Lake Nasser when the Aswan High Dam was being built in the 1960s. The rescue was planned by UNESCO. Less well known sites in northeast Africa include the 4th-century-CE obelisk of Axum, returned to Ethiopia in 2005 after it was carried off to Italy in 1937. Another Ethiopian site is Lalibela, the site of 13 medieval chuches hewn from solid rock.

North Africa's glories also include the medieval mosques and the markets or souks of cities, from Cairo in the east to Marrakech or Fez in the west. Even the sweltering wilderness of the Sahara desert has its treasures – 4,000-year-old rock paintings at Tassili n'Ajjer in Algeria.

Central and southern Africa

South of the Sahara desert, the chief building materials used to be mud, thatch and wood – practical but not durable. In Mali, there is the 15th-century trading town of Timbuktu, the Grand Mosque at Djenné (1907) and the traditional thatched huts, shaped like witches' hats, of the Dogon people. The perfection of the thatched hut tradition may be seen in the 19th-century palace tombs of the Buganda kings, at Kampala, Uganda.

A kind of coral cement was a popular building material down East Africa's Swahili coast, where Africans, Arabs and Persians traded in the Middle Ages. Mosques and dwellings with ornately carved wooden doors may be seen on islands such as Lamu in Kenya, and Zanzibar in Tanzania. The most famous stone-built building in southern Africa is Great Zimbabwe, the remains of a walled citadel which dates back to the 12th century.

Wonders of western Asia

The world's first civilizations grew up in western Asia. In Iran, one may see the ruins of Persepolis, the glorious

The Kinkaku temple, 'Golden Pavilion', (1398) in Kyoto, Japan

capital of the Persian empire in 518BCE. Petra in Jordan is a hidden city in the desert, carved from sandstone cliffs during the 1st century CE. Sana'a in Yemen has unique houses and mosques that were built from the 7th to the 11th centuries. In the mountainous Cappadocia region of Turkey there are fascinating underground towns and villages and mazes of rock-hewn passages that date back to the 4th century.

The fabulous heritage sites of western Asia have faced a number of dangers from very different directions in recent years. Jerusalem, a holy city to Jews, Muslims and Christians, is split by the violent political and religious divides that afflict Israel. The ancient clay-built citadel of Bam, in Iran, was destroyed by an earthquake in 2003. And the Iraq War, which began in 2003, has already placed many ancient and valuable Mesopotamian sites at risk.

The Alhambra, 'Red Castle', (1248–1354), in Granada, Spain

Central Asia and the steppes

The Central Asian steppes, deserts and mountains were home to nomadic peoples who had no permanent home, but moved around according to the seasons. Their tents left little trace on the landscape. However, along the ancient trading routes from China to the west there grew up wealthy cities such as Samarkand, now in Uzbekistan, and famed for its medieval mosques and observatory.

An example of the risks to monuments in Central Asia occurred in Afghanistan's fascinating Bamyan valley in 2001, when the Taliban government blew up two gigantic statues of the Buddha with explosives.

South Asian heritage

Travel southwards from Afghanistan to Pakistan, and here you will find sites such as the ancient ruins of Mohenjo Daro (2500–1500BCE), a city built by the Indus Valley civilization. In Lahore are the Shalimar Gardens and the Lahore Fort (1566). India is a large country with many treasures. At Ajanta, in the Deccan, 28 Buddhist cave temples were carved from rock between the 2nd century BCE and the 7th century CE. They were adorned with stone carvings and paintings. Southern India has many Hindu sites, such as the marvel of Konarak, a 13th-century temple to the sun god Surya. This was buried in sand for two centuries.

Traditional problems facing South Asian sites have included the hot climate, the monsoon rains and dense vegetation. More recent poblems include road-building and the spread of towns, and also an increase in tourism in, for example, Sri Lankan cities such as Kandy.

East Asian marvels

China has many heritage sites. In Beijing are the Temple of Heaven and the old Imperial Palace, with its 800 halls (both built in 1420). In Xian, there is the underground mausoleum of the first Chinese emperor, Qin Shi Huang, with a lifelike army modelled in terracotta buried in 210BCE. At Leshan is a colossus, a 71m-high Buddha carved from a cliff face between 713 and 803CE. Many Chinese temples were damaged in during a period of political unrest in the 1960s. However, many of these have now been restored.

Japan is known for ultra-modern cities, but Kyoto has splendid shrines of the Shinto religion. In North Korea are tombs from the ancient kingdom of Koguryo, and in South Korea are many shrines and palaces. Thailand's historic city of Ayutthaya (1351) is marked by towers and Buddhist monasteries. Indonesia's marvels include the 1,200-year-old Buddhist temple of Borobodur, on the island of Java.

North America old and new

North America is fixed in our minds as a relatively modern continent. There are buildings from the 15th-century early colonization by English and Spanish settlers, and historic

The standing stones of Stonehenge, England (2500–2000BCE)

centres in the old French cities including Québec in Canada and New Orleans in Louisiana in the United States. However, our imagination is also captivated by the 'American dream' – the great skyscrapers of the cities, or modern colossi such as the heads of four presidents carved on Mount Rushmore in South Dakota between 1927 and 1941.

Many sites in North America date back to an earlier age, to the Native American cultures that once dominated this continent. One important world heritage site is at Mesa Verde in the state of Colorado, where pueblo-style dwellings built between the 6th and 12th centuries cling to the sides of cliffs.

Mexico and Central America

The most developed pre-Columbian (Aztec, Olmec and Mayan) civilizations grew up further to the south, where great cities, such as the Aztec capital of Tenochtitlán (on the site of modern Mexico City), were built. There are many astounding archaeologial sites in this region – for example, Monte Albán in Mexico, or the Mayan sites of Palenque in Mexico and Copán in Honduras.

Lost cities of South America

Great stone arches and walls may still be seen at Tiwanaku in Bolivia (600–1200), and they are testament to the many ancient civilizations of South America. Chan Chan (850–1470), on the Peruvian coast, was capital of the Chimü kingdom, and at its height, had a population of 30,000. The former capital of the Inca empire was at Cuzco in Peru. One of the world's most exciting heritage sites is the 15th-century fortress town of Machu Picchu in Peru, which clings to twin mountain peaks in the high Andes Mountains. This is the lost city of the Incas, forgotten for centuries by the outside world.

Across the Pacific

On the Pacific islands, we find traces of Polynesian and other cultures, including the statues of Easter Island. In Australia, most of the heritage sites are natural wonders – rainforests and deserts. Yet these too were sites of great significance to the Aboriginal peoples who lived there for tens of thousands of years before the arrival of Europeans. Trees, creeks and boulders were for them like temples or shrines, sacred marks in a landscape. The most famous such site is Uluru, also known as Ayer's Rock.

Many of the civilizations featured in this book tried to compete with the wonders of nature by building towers, pyramids and skyscrapers. The Australian Aborigines were content with the real wonder of the world – the force of nature. As we explore the older sites of world heritage, we find that common inspirations and skills unite humanity. However, we also find a rich variety and diversity of cultures. Every people and region once had their own unique styles of architecture. One reason for this was practical. Building materials varied according to the local climate and the available raw materials. Modern wonders, by comparison, are generally constructed in a uniform global syle. A modern dam looks impressive, but it appears much the same whether it is in Tajikistan or Brazil. The variety of styles through the ages makes the conservation of historical world heritage sites all the more important. Our past will inform and influence our present.

Machu Picchu, high in the Andes Mountains of Peru

Glossary

amphitheatre
A building containing an arena for sports or combat, surrounded by raised seating.

aqueduct
A channel built to carry water, often supported by a bridge.

archaeologist
Someone who investigates and studies ancient ruins and remains.

ball court
The playing area for a sacred ball game played by the ancient peoples of Mexico and Central America.

Discus thrower, ancient Greece

beam bridge
A bridge which has a rigid horizontal deck that is supported by piers.

cable-stayed bridge
A type of beam bridge in which the deck is supported by piers but also secured by steel cables.

cenote (pronounced sen-aw-teh)
A sunken pool in limestone rock, found in Mexico and Central America.

chacmool
The stone statue of a reclining figure, found at several ancient sites in Mexico and Central America and possibly used during human sacrifice.

clan
A social group made up of people claiming descent from a common ancestor.

colossus *plural* **colossi**
Any gigantic statue, such as the Colossus of Rhodes.

computer modelling
Using computer calculations to test whether certain options will work, for example in planning a building.

conservation
Protecting and caring for an environment or a site.

culture
1 Any way of living, its customs and traditions. **2** Creative activities such as music, art or literature.

deck
The horizontal section of a bridge, generally supporting a road or railway.

flood barrier
A means of protecting coastlines or river banks from flooding, often using steel gates that can be raised temporarily.

galley
A large ship which can be propelled by long oars.

gladiator
In ancient Rome, someone trained to fight in the arena for entertainment.

Carving from Angkor Wat

heritage
Something inherited by a generation from its ancestors, such as a fine building or a way of life.

hydroelectric power
Electric power generated from the motion of water.

Industrial Revolution
The rise of new technology and production methods in the 18th and 19th centuries.

information technology
Practical methods of storing and retrieving information.

Internet
Electronic communication through a series of computer networks.

irrigation
Methods of bringing water to dry land in order to grow crops.

mausoleum
Any monumental tomb, named after the original Mausoleum of Halicarnassus.

Mesopotamia
The lands around the rivers Tigris and Euphrates, now occupied by Iraq and parts of Syria and Iran.

moai
Huge stone heads carved and raised by Polynesians on Easter Island.

mythology
A system of belief that seeks to explain creation and the natural world through stories about gods, spirits, demons, heroes or animals.

nuclear particles
Tiny specks of matter to be found in the core or nucleus of an atom.

pharaoh
A ruler of ancient Egypt, thought by the Egyptians to be a god on Earth.

pier
1 A platform that projects into a river or sea. **2** A long pillar that supports a structure such as a bridge.

pile
A strong pole of timber, concrete or metal driven into rock or a riverbed to support a structure such as a building.

pollution
The poisoning of air, land or water by waste or chemicals.

pyramid
A monument with a square base, and sides that converge to a point at the top.

relief
A carving, generally in stone or clay, that stands out from its background, giving it a three-dimensional appearance.

Renaissance
'Rebirth' – the period of heightened cultural activity that arose in Europe in the 15th and 16th centuries.

solar panel
An array of cells used to generate electricity from the energy of the sun.

space telescope
A spacecraft with a telescope, sent into orbit as an observatory.

sphinx
A beast with the body of a lion and the head of human, found in Egyptian mythology. There is a famous sphinx that guards one of the three pyramids at Giza.

steppes
The rolling grasslands of southern Europe and Central Asia.

stepped pyramid
A pyramid with layered sections rather than flat sides.

suspension bridge
A bridge that has a deck which is supported by suspended cables.

surveyor
Someone who measures the lie of the land before the construction of a road, bridge or building.

technology
The ways in which science can be applied for practical ends, such as metalworking, mining or electronics.

temple
A site of religious ritual or worship. The term is used in various religions including Hinduism, Buddhism, Judaism and the ancient beliefs of western Asia, and Central and South America.

turbine
An engine whose spinning blades are turned by currents of air or water in order to generate power.

tsunami
A gigantic, powerful ocean wave, usually created by an earthquake or undersea volcanic eruption.

viaduct
Any bridge with unusually high piers, designed to carry road or rail.

wind tunnel
A tube in which models of planned buildings or aircraft are tested in a steady current of air, to see how they will react to air currents and stresses.

wonders of the world
Originally, a list of the seven most marvellous sights to be seen in the world, as drawn up by various writers in ancient Greece and medieval Europe.

World Wide Web
A system of linking up information sources across computer networks.

ziggurat
A massive sacred monument found in ancient Mesopotamian cities, a sort of stepped pyramid.

The Hubble Space Telescope (HST)

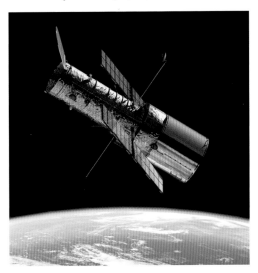

Index

Acknowledgements

The publisher would like to thank the following for permission to reproduce their material. Every care has been taken to trace copyright holders. However, if there have been unintentional omissions or failure to trace copyright holders, we apologize and will, if informed, endeavour to make corrections in any future edition.

Key: *b* = bottom, *c* = centre, *l* = left, *r* = right, *t* = top

Cover *l* Photolibrary; Cover *c* Corbis Tim Graham; pages *1* Getty Images National Geographic Society; 2–3 Photolibrary JtB Photo Communications; 4–5 Panoramic Images; 8*l* Alamy Werner Otto; 8*r* Corbis Christine Osbourne; 10 Mary Evans Picture Library; 12*cl* Stephane Compoint; 12*b* Stephane Compoint; 13*t* Stephane Compoint; 13*b* Corbis Kin Cheung; 14 Corbis Nik Wheeler; 15 Bridgeman Art Library British Museum; 16 Bridgeman Art Library Private Collection; 17 Werner Forman Archive; 18 Bridgeman Art Library Private Collection; 20 *tl* Art Archive Dagli Orti; 20*c* Stephane Compoint; 21 Stephane Compoint; 22 Bridgeman Art Library Private Collection; 24–25 Alamy Arco Images; 25*tr* Corbis Tom Brakefield; 26–27 Photolibrary Panorama Media; 26*b* Empics AP; 27*tr* Getty Images Imagebank; 28–29*b* Photolibrary Jon Arnold Images; 28 Heritage Images Partnership; 28–29*t* Corbis Kevin R. Morris; 29*r* Photolibrary Photononstop; 30*l* Corbis Keren Su; 30–31 Getty Images Taxi; 31*t* Corbis Douglas Peebles; 32*bl* Getty Images Stone; 32*c* Art Archive Dagli Orti; 32*tr* Corbis Ludovic Maisant; 33 Getty Images National Geographic Society; 34*tl* Bridgeman Art Library Private Collection; 34*tr* Alamy Steve Allen Travel Photography; 34–35 Impact Photos Yann Arthus-Bertrand; 35*br* Corbis Jim Zuckerman; 36–37 Getty Images Panoramic Images; 36*t* Corbis Jonathan Blair; 37*r* Empics AP; 38 Corbis Keren Su; 40–41 Getty Images Taxi; 41*t* Corbis Bettmann; 42 Photolibrary Index Stock Imagery; 43*t* Photolibrary; 43*b* Corbis Charles & Josette Lenars; 44*tr* Alamy Mike Goldwater; 44*b* Getty Images Hulton; 45 Photolibrary Mary Plage; 46–47 Corbis Reuters; 46*b* Construction Photography; 48*t* Rex Features; 48*b* Photolibrary Dynamics Graphics; 49 Corbis Robert Harding Photo Library; 50–51 Corbis Richard T. Nowitz; 51 Corbis Gail Mooney; 52 NASA/ESA; 52–53 NASA; 53 NASA/ESA; 54 Photolibrary Index Stock Imagery; 55*tl* Corbis Free Agents Ltd; 55*br* Photolibrary Index Stock Imagery; 56*tr* Getty Images Photonica; 56*b* Alamy Rolf Richardson; 57 Getty Images Lonely Planet; 58*tl* Getty Images Imagebank; 58*cr* Photolibrary Jon Arnold Images; 59 Getty Images Taxi; 60*l* Stephane Compoint; 60–61*t* Corbis Kevin R. Morris; 61*r* NASA/ESA; 64 Getty Images Stone